Praise for Into My Garden

"These remarkable poems blend spiritual unease with religious confidence, an investigator's fascinated spirit with a sense that the poet has almost—but not quite—come home. Caplan writes to portray this Orthodox Jewish world as a set of real people with serious joys and concerns, neither figures for trouble elsewhere (the land of Israel never appears) nor idealized Others from an ancestral past. Other poets have made American poems from Jewish interpretive traditions; Caplan stands out in that he makes poems about the present-day people who try to live by those traditions. Caplan's lines try to bring into their pace and their phrasing, their details given and withheld, a way of life that he shares in part, and stands outside in part, and has brought into his circumspect and introspective American English. This project of sympathy with the yeshiva students never seems more successful than when Caplan shares their joys: the third person of 'Chassidus by Telephone,' asking 'To get religious—what does that mean?' might be somebody the poet observes 'on the train home' or it might be the poet himself, without an epiphany or a 'wonder story,' who nonetheless finds that 'a lecture on fear and love' has become 'a wordless tune,' an experience at once aesthetic, sociable, discursive, and religious, a credible form of communal sacred song."
—**Stephanie Burt**

"David Caplan's Into My Garden gives us a series of evocative poems that ask the big questions—about faith, doubt, love, yearning, and, most powerfully of all, the yearning for knowledge. Caplan also debates the basis of the big questions, asking 'To know/what you feel, not what you ought to feel,/is there anything harder?' Poems set in a yeshiva school, where emulation and interpretation are prized, introduce a speaker who thrives through inquiry and debate. The later poems renegotiate early teachings with the realities of adulthood. In this way, Caplan is a neo-Romantic, his poetry keenly in tune with the child's unique worldview, seeing many things for the first time, before assimilated into the workings of grown-up societal norms. Into My Garden is a beautifully earnest, smart, and tender book. Caplan writes wonderfully about wonder."
—**Denise Duhamel**

"Yes, this is a book of yeshiva study, yeshiva days and nights, and of the avid, ardent, on-fire (and sometimes doubtful and conflicted) longing to understand God's Holy Words in a world of prayerful devotion where 'each syllable / [is] said corrected or repeated until it is.' But to consign these poems solely to the realm of 'religion' or 'theology' or 'scholarly exegesis' is to dismiss Rabbi Schneur Zalman's observation, 'We must live with the times.' A microphone clipped to a lapel is here, and a bodega, and a hotel lobby where 'a woman tells a stranger what she will do / for three hundred dollars.' Steeped in Ashkenazic tradition though it is, INTO MY GARDEN asks to be true to all dances and struggles—of faith as well as of flesh—of this Earth."
—**Albert Goldbarth**

"A searing, shimmering lucidity: among its many offerings, David Caplan's INTO MY GARDEN delicately, precisely, unforgettably tracks the fear and love informing Jewish study and longing. One encounters here an unusual sensibility—profound, thoughtful, rigorous, tender.

Caplan's beautifully measured lines and stanzas conjure yeshivas, cemeteries, hermeneutics, a particular beach, the life of trees, remembered friendships. From Chasidic scholars to Ezra Pound, from Queens to Jerusalem, Caplan addresses complex inheritances and uncertain movements toward the holy. The erotics of prayer, of ritual; the stringencies and ambiguities of interpretation; an ongoing testing of self and of religious engagement; the status of memory; hopes and disappointments in marriage—Caplan's horizons are both vast and intimate. This is a book both of these times and not: beautiful and occasionally painful distillations of a notably searching intelligence and heart. An assured, commanding book which has its sights on something far more important than the merely literary."
—**Maureen N. McLane**

"'I don't remember half / the prayers I've said, even saying them,' confides David Caplan, bringing American Confessionalism into the Chassidic tradition in this searching and luminous collection. INTO MY GARDEN teaches us 'that anger / is idolatry and world means concealment' in Jewish theology, but it also makes a yeshiva of City Park, where we learn how 'the world leans toward kindness, // God's finger on the scale.' From Ezra Pound's Venice to the Biblical Song of Songs, these poems investigate the eternal dialectic of understanding and awe. Such art is only made possible through the most disciplined of devotions: 'each syllable / said correctly or repeated until it is.'"
—**Srikanth Reddy**

"David Caplan's brilliant new collection takes us into a yeshiva, and into the searching, longing, and dedication of the student mind. As he writes in INTO MY GARDEN, 'The more/ you need them, the more words demand.' I close this book thinking deeply not only about faith but also about language—how, whether in poetry or in prayer, it carries us, guides us toward understanding."
—**Maggie Smith**

"These elliptical, imagistic, and lovely poems arrive at the perfect pitch for honoring the inexplicable—in its tragic, lifting, and mystical iterations. While rooted deeply in Chassidic faith and culture, Caplan's masterful poetry does not spare the reader painful questions, personal sorrows, an aching sense of alienation. INTO MY GARDEN accomplishes what many concerned with contemporary poetry deem impossible: a book of devotional poems that speaks poignantly, often heartbreakingly, to the believers and nonbelievers of our present moment. This brilliant book is a treasure of the Chassidic—and the human—experience."
—**Yehoshua November**

"The value of Caplan's work is not anthropological; it is literary and psychological. He has rendered the complex inner experience of becoming a contemporary Hasid in decidedly un-Hasidic language. Indeed, Caplan's poems are powerful and surprising, in part, because they are written in the familiar introspective and confessional first-person voice of late-modern American lyric poetry."

"...the spiritual experience he describes will be familiar to *ba'alei teshuvah* and other spiritual seekers. The beauty of Caplan's book is that it is not polemical. It does not set out to win an argument or ask you whether you've put your tefillin on today. These gentle poems invite the reader into one person's profound, ambiguous religious experience."
—**Jake Marmer,** *Jewish Review of Books*

Into My Garden

Poems

David Caplan

Ben Yehuda Press
Teaneck, New Jersey

Into My Garden ©2020 David Caplan. All rights reserved. No part of this book may be used or reproduced in any manner whatsoever without written permission except in the case of brief quotations embodied in critical articles and reviews.

Published by Ben Yehuda Press
122 Ayers Court #1B
Teaneck, NJ 07666

http://www.BenYehudaPress.com

Jewish Poetry Project #13
http://jpoetry.us

To subscribe to our monthly book club and support independent Jewish publishing, visit https://www.patreon.com/BenYehudaPress

ISBN13 978-1-934730-88-1
cover photograph by Noah Rabinowitz.

Poems in this book have appeared in the following publications (some in different form):
At Length: "Too Young to Slice Peppers" and "On a Late Photograph of Ezra Pound"
New England Review: "Grateful" (titled as "Since Sleep is One-Sixtieth of Death")
Poetry Magazine: "In a Hotel"
Virginia Quarterly Review: "Into My Garden," "Only the Hebrew," "God Knows English," "The Mistake," "Alien Fire," "Nittel Nacht," "Before the City" (titled as "Ohel"), "Chassidus by Telephone," "Bris Milah," "Bound" "After," "Causeway," and "Fisherman's Beach"
32 Poems: "City Park, March or April," section V.
Southwest Review, "This World is Just"
upstreet: "Memory halves whatever it touches…,"

I would like to thank the editors the *Virginia Quarterly Review* who awarded Emily Clark Balch Prize for Poetry to a group of these poems (then titled "Observances").

I have come into My garden, My sister, My bride.

The Song of Songs

Contents

Into My Garden	1
Only the Hebrew	2
God Knows English	3
The Mistake	4
Alien Fire	5
The Last Class	6
Even the Thief	7
Tikvah Way	8
Into My Garden (II)	9
Nittel Nacht	10
Flashcards	11
Night Run	12
Old Recording	13
Before the City	14
Chassidus by Telephone	15
Into My Garden (III)	16
Gorilla Suit	17
Neilah	18
Bris Milah	19
After	20

II
In a Hotel	23
This World is Just	24
Sarah Overhearing the Angel's Blessing	25
Too Young to Slice Peppers	26
Grateful	27
Second Seder, Atlanta	28
Rachel	29
Before the City, Again	30

III
Dear Yehoshua	35
On a Late Photograph of Ezra Pound	37
Causeway	43
Fisherman's Beach	44
City Park, March or April	45
Memory halves whatever it touches . . .	50
Day and night, night and day . . .	51
New Song	52
Notes	55
About the Author	57

Into My Garden

As if New Jersey were Babylon, an Argentine
and an Israeli argue in Aramaic, Styrofoam cups
of instant coffee warm in their hands.

Other boys return to last night's commentary:
I have come into My garden,
back and forth they sing like an invitation.

What did I learn in school? Whenever
the philosopher lectured on the death of metaphysics,
pollen found an open window, pistil

and stamen crazed with each other.
Yellow, the serpentine walls and columns.
Yellow, the library where a church belonged.

Some nights his best student recited
the lecture like a pledge, but nothing changed ,
not the pitcher between us, the glass

slick with our fingerprints, the envy I felt.
Boys dressed like men race the stairwell as if to the singing,
as if to hear what *My garden* means:

seven generations caused God to withdraw,
seven generations drew him back.
All those years of talking—what did I learn?

Only the Hebrew

The sudden quiet of a room emptied of noise.
Only the Hebrew, a stone on his tongue.

The boy who carried his suitcase up the stairs
swayed as if into a thought.

What is holy? No walls of Jerusalem stone,
no microphone discreetly clipped across a lapel

to announce when to stand. The more
you need them, the more words demand.

Windowsills honored with books,
pictures of the righteous, watching.

God Knows English

You know how certain singers turn words
into sounds, keeping only the tune?
Clean-shaven, hatless, he waited

for the opposite to happen.
God knows English, he wanted to say,
wanted to leave the old books

open to the same page, each line
read aloud for him to repeat, each syllable.
Easy to let a beard claim your face

like a sign of knowledge, easy
to wait for the afternoon to end.
In the study hall's thin electric light,

he listened to them scat sing,
the commentary hooked and curved
as if released from sense.

The Mistake

No mirrors, not even above the sink,
only the study hall's glass doors
repeating the mistake that each is the same,

one reflection bending into the next,
students and teachers alike abstracted
into the same outline of a dark suit and hat,

but to repent is to see again,
notice the sly shrugs and alliances,
as each defends his answer

against the others' challenges,
the Aramaic checked on smart phones,
quickened into English, Spanish, and Hebrew.

Alien Fire

Late Saturday afternoon, late winter,
they sway and clap, not wanting
to let the chorus go, and when their teacher asks,

What are you, dead?, a boy
jumps onto the table, his best shoes
finding plastic cups and leftovers,

and another takes a friend onto his back,
as if spinning in circles, faster and tighter,
answered the question. To run to God

and return: when you close your eyes and sing,
know the first boy atop the table
yesterday taught a prisoner how to pray

and tonight will wait in line to swab
the inside of his cheek because he heard
a Jew somewhere is sick.

The Last Class

The philosopher shrugged when we applauded
and the lecture hall emptied except for us,
flirting and waiting—for what?

A sense that we are saved from the wrongness,
the philosopher's favorite philosopher called religion,
but wasn't that what we wanted,

to read the books our teachers had read
so our questions would sound like theirs,
knowing and not too eager?

*We shall never be in touch with something
greater than ourselves,* the philosopher's
best student impersonated him perfectly,

the same short stutter between "shall" and "never,"
the same gaze at some point beyond us.

Even the Thief

A night of snow no one expected.
This late the study hall sounds different,
the same words said again, dark and glowing,
a window scratched with its mistakes.
Everyone knows God controls the universe,
my study-partner translates without a pause.
Even the thief prays for success. To know
what you feel, not what you ought to feel,
is there anything harder? At the airport,
a man with The Book of Genesis
tattooed down his leg boarded in front of me,
and I couldn't help but wonder how it would feel
to have those words that close.

Tikvah Way

He remembers the golf course's last hill,
how it felt to sprint it. Even then,
he knew how little it mattered,

the slogans his coaches shouted,
how much they cared.
They would still recognize his stride.

When the widower he visits
each Friday repeats the transliterated
blessing, word by word,

the vowels open into themselves.
It shouldn't be this hard,
up the long driveway each

breath insists before it relents.

Into My Garden (II)

All week they studied what he is about to say.
Born after his death, they want more than stories,
want to feel how it felt to be in that room,
stand with the old men he blessed for long life and listen.

Under the white tablecloth, a handkerchief
wrapped around his hand bound his soul.
I have come into My garden, My sister, My bride . . .
Projected across the study hall, downloaded
and captioned, he closes his eyes and explains.

Nittel Nacht

To separate, we say when comparing
unlike things, like our Bibles and the Bibles
that missionaries stacked along the driveway.

The morning we found them everyone had a story,
remembering a stranger in a check-out line,
smiling as if at a shared joke: *I love Jews*,

but I thought of the deer who saw me
cut through his woods,
not hunted for generations, indifferent.

To separate: the same thing understood
differently as in a false translation.
To separate, the actor always

tears a certain page from the hotel Bible,
otherwise he cannot sleep.
December 24th, the study hall knows

only chessboards, little plastic kings
that add nothing to their night.

Flashcards

A picnic table spiked with shade. The flashcards
he shuffles rework yesterday's mistakes,
the root and tense of what the mystics knew:
the soul descends into this world so longing

can accomplish what revelation cannot,
longing and distance. *Answer us,*
a fist against the heart, one beat for each sin.
Make this world make sense.

Night Run

A night run so he can sleep
as if it could sweep him clean
like the bodega he sprints past—another
grated window that gives little back,
his body too faint to discern, passing.

Old Recording

I know how to pray but not like this—

in the old recording, he repeats the blessings
we repeat three times a day,

his familiar accent and cadence, urgent and assured,
naming what is missing when I say

the same words, the certain knowledge
that each word needs to be said.

Before the City

> Montefiore Cemetery,
> Cambria Heights, Queens

The need to be heard does not change,
the need to get close. Again we tear
our request, scatter it across the grave.

The first time we came we only knew
what to ask for, not what to do: knock
before entering to clear some room,

fast before knocking. Before the city,
before the slow time of waiting,
stones crown the two tombstones,

a wedding invitation spotted with rain,
letter after letter read aloud.
Just as the righteous are greater in death,

a marriage without children counts
backward, the gray light measuring
a skyline of torn paper, white stone.

Chassidus by Telephone

On the train home, a Bluetooth in his ear,
he listens to a lecture on fear and love,
the four kinds, lower and higher.
To get religious—what does that mean?

Sometimes it all feels like an improvisation:
the snow lifting from the tracks,
a hardboiled egg wrapped in foil, an extra
sandwich in case he meets someone who needs it.

He has no wonder story to tell, no moment
where a miracle resolved all doubt,
only a classroom after the term's last class.
Love and fear: a wordless tune

sung faster and louder,
as if that were the reason
the soul descended into this world,
to link arms with friends and sing.

Into My Garden (III)

The true meaning is allegorical
and the literal meaning is false—
so they translate the Songs of Songs

with allegory as the primary meaning,
as if to show us how to avoid
misunderstanding whatever we see.

Two teenage girls straddling a stone wall
curved like the expressway out of the city:
they watch each other, nothing else.

Gorilla Suit

The last day of class, the novelist
threw bananas from atop his desk.
Drunk, of course, inside his gorilla suit,
but wasn't he right, if the novels
we read could be trusted?
Scratching himself, he bellowed:
Life is just a bunch of bananas.
Friends, get 'em while you can!

Neilah

Last year's words sour in our mouths, useless:
last year's failures.

Rain claws the roof.
Embarrassed to be heard, we need

to be answered. Too late for good manners,
each prayer jostles to break free.

Bris Milah

For Menachem Mendel Schottenstein

Across Eastern Parkway the camera
      recognized his walk,
neither absent minded nor harried.

Alone, he did not run his hand
      along a neighbor's
brick wall. Only the maples' top branches

acknowledged spring, holding it
      like a secret. A taxi
sped downtown. How little is seen:

a fedora's crown pinched on both sides,
      the brim bent down,
an ordinary black overcoat and beard.

This is what *covenant* means: each night
      he carries home
a briefcase no more than a brown paper sack

stuffed with names to pray for.
      Menachem Mendel,
may you learn your namesake's walk.

After

> We must live with the times.
> —Rabbi Schneur Zalman of Liadi

Each morning I skim the books they study,
a few minutes to remember that anger

is idolatry and *world* means concealment.
And when someone slaps the lectern

and the prayers start, I try not to think
of what comes after: sunlight

angling against the cars angling
against each other. In the study hall,

an hour to prepare, an hour to ask:
Live with the times, what does that mean?

To make my flight, I prayed early
as if the room were empty:

walls of books I had not read, the teacher
adding a question to yesterday's answer.

David Caplan

II

In a Hotel

In a hotel, even prayer feels adulterous,
the skyline smudged in light, a distraction
just before dusk. In the lobby

a woman tells a stranger what she will do
for three hundred dollars, what
she will do for four. Some have the custom

of opening a book randomly with a question in mind.
Some have the custom of forgetting.
At six my friend beat his father at chess,

beat his father's friends so easily
he wondered if they tried.
At seven he shook the Governor's hand.

Don't call it a failure; call it knowledge:
the peculiar taste that filled his mouth
as if he had bitten his cheek.

Whatever he risked did not matter, whatever
he could imagine was already lost.
Bored, the other boy coughed into his hands.

This World is Just

Dumpster flies taste the sweet in the bitter.
They know the world is just,
sunlit and oily after a noon rain.

Inside the portico, dry cool shade.
A nurse waves ash into a coffee can,
the filter of her cigarette neatly snapped off.

Just as a reset bone never forgets the insult,
patients and visitors alike walk as if across ash.
Wrong to call them *shrieks* or *grunts*,

wrong to say *delusions*. How many psalms
have been recited in this room patiently as a lullaby,
how many nights has her daughter slept

on a fold-out cot as if she were a child again,
giving up her room for a guest?
Look how much kindness, she says

my mother brings into this world.

Sarah Overhearing the Angel's Blessing

> And he [the angel] said,
> "I will return to you next year
> and Sarah, your wife, will have a son."
> —Genesis 18:10

A small painting, darkly lit and rarely shown,
as if it were best not to see Sarah laugh
at the promise all her sadness will soon end.
Best not to see what she is thinking,
best to keep it private. Isn't that why God
lies to Abraham, lies for the sake of peace?
Best not to say what we know:
everyone is either a parent or a child,
whether sketched in chiaroscuro or listening
to a doctor apologize for what is already known.
Best not to see it, darkly lit and small, doubled back
like candles in a mirror, the humiliation
of a marriage without children, the slow time of waiting.

Too Young to Slice Peppers

Too young to slice peppers,
our niece points whenever
a hummingbird finds the feeder.

Glass doors explain the balcony,
apartments named for an orange grove,
mistranslated into Spanish.

If sleep is one-sixtieth of death,
what percentage of life is memory?
Again the grandfather

she calls forgetful cups his palm
into a nest, whistles to the bird
he just named until she laughs.

O little one, O my forever.

Grateful

Grateful, always the day's first word,
the first word of the first prayer,
mumbled like an apology. Today it means

We still have clients, though they can't pay.
Just past the fountain a runner presses
two fingers to his throat and feels

how quickly his blood grows stupid,
how it forgets ten circuits around the city's
best park, timed on a wristwatch.

Second Seder, Atlanta

Three a.m., three thirty. Down Christmas Lane,
down Holly and Merry, houses are lit with singing.
He is great, He is wise, He is King.

Each stanza the epithets change but not the chorus
because that it is how praise and desire work.
Quickly, quickly, rebuild Your House.

The night's symbols have performed their obligations:
the eggs smooth with salt water, the unleavened bread,
the pillows we lean into like a question.

If what we pray for happened today, who would leave
this giant table, our best napkins pink with wine?
Crumbs in our mouths, who would stay?

Rachel

Give me children. If not, I will die, Rachel pled,
And from here we learn, Rashi adds,
a childless person is considered dead,
as if we did not know how it feels
to say the same words three times a day
and call them prayer, in a small room, facing east,
each day a series of obligations:
what to say, what not to say, the obligation
to love and fear God, not understand Him.

Before the City, Again

>   Montefiore Cemetery,
>   Cambria Heights, Queens

A skyline of torn paper
                  measuring
a marriage

          read aloud
                spotted with rain
              two tombstones.

Before
        the city,

    clear some room,

        only

our request   across the grave,
the need

        does not change.

Into My Garden

III

Dear Yehoshua

I

A row of windows lit from inside.
Whenever I think of what I learned there,
Into My garden, My sister, My bride,
each evening the day's lessons
stepping back, just out of reach,
Into My garden, My sister, My bride,
instead, I remember everyone
dancing to welcome the Sabbath, breaking
off into circles then back into one,
Stay with me a little longer,
the two of us standing just a little apart.

II

This early we translate each sentence twice
so we can hear it once: how the soul
is commanded the same as Abraham,

"Go forth from your land, your birthplace,
and your father's house." This early,
your family is asleep, my wife asleep,

only the city, lit and waiting, the black
water giving nothing back, no sunlight or shade,
nothing from the sky. Too early to pray,

we try to understand what was obvious
to those who wrote the prayers we will say.
Is this my life, do you also wonder,

the soul sent down against its will
to accomplish a task never revealed to it,
hurrying from one mistake to the next,
daydreaming about God?

On a Late Photograph of Ezra Pound

Taken in Venice, 1964

I

Late afternoon, chiaroscuro is needed, a long
sentence where the old man can wait.
I have invented nothing, not his hand

on the white stone, his ivory-handled walking stick.
Inside, saints, pained and accusatory,
protest the temporary light a few coins

bring to their faces. Inside, another
master flays a murderer, opens him
like a riddle. I have invented nothing,

not how the old man blinked twice
to mean "no," not the excuses
he left for his widow and mistress.

Buon giorno, maestro. If he did not answer,
the shopkeepers understood.
In the empty square, the old man hunched

into himself, the old desire to insult
the world, the pillar's cracked base.

II

More of what he hated, less of what was loved:
whether a round at the Gritti or another war
to finance a war—everyone buys on credit,

except the sunlight each walks into down the Zattere,
the shopkeeper's long broom, the back of a tapestry,
and each awning ending in sunlight,

as if the doge's men had stolen sunlight, not bones.

III

Bad teeth, bad prostate, no matter. White chested,
the old man feels the clouds make way.

Memory, go back that birdsong: tenors called up from the army,
like violinists behind a grille, in and out of sight.

The right idea can skip centuries like an aria,
but someone must work for it.

Some must sell tickets. Someone must explain
two hundred concerti forgotten like a cough.

Liberty is still a duty, not a right,
no matter how many statues are smashed with pikes.

IV

Why should tidewater respect the schedule of tides,
apologize for its own history and desires?

Let them build gangways. Let them take precautions.
"You wouldn't understand it. Most people don't,"

he told the girl the chaplain brought,
who said she wrote poetry but hadn't read his.

What was she, twelve? A pigeon with a taste for marble,
let her hear and remember how she pecked

at his throat and the sound that came out,
black wind scraping a chimney:

"A kike as well as a cunt. Give up poetry."
Alone in a fold-out chair, waiting . . .

When he talked of his friends, it began to rain.
One would dance with him for what he might say.

V Ghetto Nuovo

Cameras angled from inside their jackets,
they've come to photograph ghosts hurrying into abstraction.

Would it matter if they knew I also am a tourist?
An hour before dusk, sunlight tests the barred windows

and a couple bending into the synagogue's doorway
thanks the guard who checked their passports.

VI Afterimage: Olga

After twenty years of hustlers drinking her tea,
        what is quieter than a gallery in winter,
                the little girl healed by her father's candle,

as if that were all it took, the right words prayed over
        her, the right light? Old tricks govern the mud: piles
        keep the pitched world level.

Since gossips believe only their stories, she'll give them
        the right words, the right light.
                "Suffering exists to make people think,"

he wrote in Italian so their daughter would learn.
        Understand? The visitor nods, again.
                It is garbage, but she believes it.

Unwed widow, the door still bears her name.

Causeway

A steeple repainted with a Star of David,
the street still named for a saint —

I don't remember half
the prayers I've said, even saying them,
the words I mumbled, quoting God,

distracted by the person beside me,
swaying into his prayers,
or distracted by the room's stillness
that repeats like a complaint.

Any more is fanaticism,
any less heresy. Open water
on one side, the bay on the other,
a beagle leashed to a bench
yelps for the beach
as if showing us how it is done.

Fisherman's Beach

No tide pools, no couples on the beach
where my parents met,

only whitecaps lifting into themselves,
bowing and lifting,

until each blurs into something else:
rocks pink with crab shells,

a workday of gulls circling trawlers,
indecipherable buoys. Walking home,

we carry this Sabbath with us,
carry it like gossip, the old prophesies

read aloud and followed
across the page, each syllable

said correctly or repeated until it is.

City Park, March or April

I

Boys play basketball. Nothing sly or easy,
no smooth stutter steps, no cuts
to where the ball will be thrown.
They haven't yet learned how to move.

II

Eight men drag a corpse down the streets.
Friends, they ride slowly, two to a motorcycle,
into the blessings the crowd shouts.

They burned him and broke his jaw and teeth.
He was hanged for forty five days by his arms and legs,
tomorrow the widow will insist. *He was no informer.*

III

All these bodies smeared with sunlight,
faces, breasts, and legs,
as if bodies were made only for that,
to touch and be touched—

IV

A priest blessed a man on crutches.
Cripples knelt to pray. In the Christmas display,
Styrofoam streaked gray and black

retold the history of rubble,
the cathedral just outside the train station,
its nave blown open into a field.

V

The boys throw back whatever they catch.
All afternoon they whistle and curse like men.

A little pond stocked for spring,
the world leans toward kindness,

God's finger on the scale. For a week
or two each year, no more,

we see it: these trees named for royalty,
each branch overwhelmed, purple and swaying.

Memory halves whatever it touches . . .

Memory halves whatever it touches:
the harbor cleared of pleasure boats,
the pier ending before the dock.

A man too small for his clothes
leans into the story he tells,
the boy beside him, listening.

The cold wet air hides their faces,
hides the streetlight on at midday,
the ocean ending at the sky.

Decades later that is all he will remember:
how everything seemed out of time.
Snow under ice, ice under salt:

look how the living walk with the dead,
each holding the other, forgetting.

Day and night, night and day . . .

my neighbor brushes his wife's hair and croons.
On their little balcony because
She likes the sun on her face, every morning

because *she understands more than she seems.*
I haven't been to a synagogue in fifty years.
What do you think about that?

Walking up the stairs after the morning services—
the same words mumbled again—
I wonder if I will ever make a sound as holy.

New Song

I

When I told the dead I didn't have any new songs to share,
disappointed, they turned away,
nimbly down the hill. Only my friend stayed,

edging close to what I might share with him.
Sunlight misquoted his face.
Don't be afraid, you are always afraid

of the wrong thing. Afraid of what?
The son and the daughter
we never had were there, watching.

Whatever names I called, they would not answer.

II

Only after my friend raised his hand for me to stop
did I realize I had been calling
my grandfather's and my grandmother's names

and the dead whose names they had been given,
the dead they never met in life.
Was that why they had circled back,

shimmering unevenly like unkempt grass?
I saw all the old names I would not pass down,
the miracle of their survival ending

somewhere in a field like this, a field of stones
returned to stone, no footpaths or psalms,
all the names and dates restored to air.

Notes

Both the title of the collection and the poems who share its title are inspired by a line from *The Song of Songs*, "I have come into My garden, My sister, My bride," as explicated in Chassidic discourses given by two Chassidic leaders: Rabbi Yosef Yitzchak Schneerson and his successor Rabbi Menachem Mendel Schneerson, titled *Basi L'Gani* (*Into My Garden*).

"Before the City" and "Before the City, Again" are set at the gravesite of Rabbi Yosef Yitzchak Schneersohn and Rabbi Menachem Mendel Schneerson in Montefiore Cemetery, Cambria Heights, Queens.

Into My Garden (II) describes the experience of yeshiva students watching a recording Rabbi Menachem Mendel Schneerson deliver a discourse. The students were born after their Rabbi Schneerson's death.

"Nittel Nacht" describes Christmas Eve, when some yeshiva students have the custom of interrupting their studies to play chess.

"Neilah" is the last service in Yom Kippur, the Jewish Day of Repentance.

"Bris Milah" refers to a ritual circumcision. The poem was written for the occasion of Menachem Mendel Schottenstein's circumcision. According to Ashkenazic tradition, newborns are named after the deceased. In this case, the boy was named after Rabbi Menachem Mendel Schneerson.

"Grateful" refers to the first prayer observant Jews say daily, while still in bed. The prayer's first word can be translated as "grateful."

"On a Late Photograph of Ezra Pound" considers the vexing, contradictory legacy of Ezra Pound. The poem is based on a photograph taken of Pound when he was living in Venice, the city where he lived with his mistress and great love, Olga Rudge, and where he died and was buried. The incident in section IV is taken from Robin Morgan's *In Saturday's Child: A Memoir*, where she recounts how Pound insulted her when she was girl.

I would like to thank Jessica Greenbaum and HL Hix for their helpful comments on the manuscript. Gregory Dowling patiently answered my questions about Venice. I could not wish for more perceptive and generous readers. Thanks also to Larry Yudelson, the editorial director of Ben Yehuda Press, Kevin Clarke, Yehuda Halper, Bob Olmstead, and of course Ana.

This book is for James Longenbach and Yehoshua November.

About the Author

David Caplan is the author of five other books of literary criticism and poetry, including *Rhyme's Challenge: Hip Hop, Poetry, and Contemporary Rhyming Culture* and *In the World He Created According to His Will*. The Charles M. Weis Professor of English at Ohio Wesleyan University, he twice served as a Fulbright lecturer in American literature and received the *Virginia Quarterly Review*'s Emily Clark Balch Prize for Poetry and an Individual Excellence Award in Criticism from the Ohio Arts Council.

The Jewish Poetry Project

Ben Yehuda Press

From the Coffee House of Jewish Dreamers: Poems of Wonder and Wandering and the Weekly Torah Portion by Isidore Century

"Isidore Century is a wonderful poet. His poems are funny, deeply observed, without pretension." — *The Jewish Week*

The House at the Center of the World: Poetic Midrash on Sacred Space by Abe Mezrich

"Direct and accessible, Mezrich's midrashic poems often tease profound meaning out of his chosen Torah texts. These poems remind us that our Creator is forgiving, that the spiritual and physical can inform one another, and that the supernatural can be carried into the everyday."
—Yehoshua November, author of *God's Optimism*

we who desire:
Poems and Torah riffs by Sue Swartz

"Sue Swartz does magnificent acrobatics with the Torah. She takes the English that's become staid and boring, and adds something that's new and strange and exciting. These are poems that leave a taste in your mouth, and you walk away from them thinking, what did I just read? Oh, yeah. It's the Bible."
—Matthue Roth, author, *Yom Kippur A Go-Go*

Open My Lips: Prayers and Poems by Rachel Barenblat

"Barenblat's God is a personal God—one who lets her cry on His shoulder, and who rocks her like a colicky baby. These poems bridge the gap between the ineffable and the human. This collection will bring comfort to those with a religion of their own, as well as those seeking a relationship with some kind of higher power."
—Satya Robyn, author, *The Most Beautiful Thing*

Words for Blessing the World: Poems in Hebrew and English by Herbert J. Levine

"These writings express a profoundly earth-based theology in a language that is clear and comprehensible. These are works to study and learn from."
—Rodger Kamenetz, author, *The Jew in the Lotus*

Shiva Moon: Poems by Maxine Silverman

"The poems, deeply felt, are spare, spoken in a quiet but compelling voice, as if we were listening in to her inner life. This book is a precious record of the transformation saying Kaddish can bring. It deserves to be read. These are works to study and learn from."
—Howard Schwartz, author, *The Library of Dreams*

is: heretical Jewish blessings and poems by Yaakov Moshe (Jay Michaelson)

"Finally, Torah that speaks to and through the lives we are actually living: expanding the tent of holiness to embrace what has been cast out, elevating what has been kept down, advancing what has been held back, reveling in questions, revealing contradictions."
—Eden Pearlstein, aka ephryme

Texts to the Holy: Poems
by Rachel Barenblat

"These poems are remarkable, radiating a love of God that is full bodied, innocent, raw, pulsating, hot, drunk. I can hardly fathom their faith but am grateful for the vistas they open. I will sit with them, and invite you to do the same."
—Merle Feld, author of A Spiritual Life.

The Sabbath Bee: Love Songs to Shabbat
by Wilhelmina Gottschalk

"Torah, say our sages, has seventy faces. As these prose poems reveal, so too does Shabbat. Here we meet Shabbat as familiar housemate, as the child whose presence transforms a family, as a spreading tree, as an annoying friend who insists on being celebrated, as a woman, as a man, as a bee, as the ocean."
—Rachel Barenblat, author, The Velveteen Rabbi's Haggadah

All the Holes Line Up: Poems and Translations
by Zackary Sholem Berger

"Spare and precise, Berger's poems gaze unflinchingly at—but also celebrate—human imperfection in its many forms. And what a delight that Berger also includes in this collection a handful of his resonant translations of some of the great Yiddish poets." —Yehoshua November, author of God's Optimism and Two World Exist

How to Bless the New Moon: The Priestess Paths Cycle and Other Poems for Queens
by Rachel Kann

"To read Rachel Kann's poems is to be confronted with the possibility that you, too, are prophet and beloved, touched by forces far beyond your mundane knowing. So, dear reader, enter into the 'perfumed forcefield' of these words—they are healing and transformative."
—Rabbi Jill Hammer, co-author of The Hebrew Priestess

Into My Garden: Prayers
by David Caplan

"The beauty of Caplan's book is that it is not polemical. It does not set out to win an argument or ask you whether you've put your tefillin on today. These gentle poems invite the reader into one person's profound, ambiguous religious experience."
—The Jewish Review of Books

Between the Mountain and the Land is the Lesson: Poetic Midrash on Sacred Community
by Abe Mezrich

"Abe Mezrich cuts straight back to the roots of the Midrashic tradition, sermonizing as a poet, rather than idealogue. Best of all, Abe knows how to ask questions and avoid the obvious answers."
—Jake Marmer, author, *Jazz Talmud*

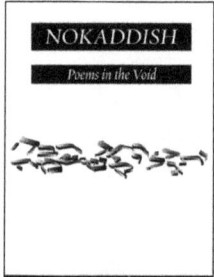

NOKADDISH: Poems in the Void
by Hanoch Guy Kaner

"A subversive, midrashic play with meanings—specifically Jewish meanings, and then the reversal and negation of these meanings."
—Robert G. Margolis

The Jewish Poetry Project
jpoetry.us

www.ingramcontent.com/pod-product-compliance
Lightning Source LLC
LaVergne TN
LVHW041346080426
835512LV00006B/632